Molokhia

The Royal Superfood

Molokhia

The Royal Superfood

Basel Nashat Asmar

2050 consulting

2050 Consulting
48 Imperial Hall
104-122 City Road
London EC1V 2NR
United Kingdom

A CIP for this book is available from the British Library.

ISBN 978-1-917915-01-4

Author's Notes:
1. The material in the book made no use of any proprietary data owned by S&P Global, and does not express S&P Global's opinion. The opinions expressed in this book are the responsibility of the author.

2. The use of particular designations of countries or territories does not imply any judgement by the author as to the legal status of such countries or territories, of their authorities and institutions or of the delimitation of their boundaries.

Printed in the United Kingdom

Cover design by Eman Faidi

To my grandmothers, whose mastery in cooking molokhia turned it into a cherished family tradition, and whose memory continues to warm our hearts with every spoonful

List of Contents

Acknowledgments

I am deeply grateful to my beloved mother Fairouz Taha Doleh,[1] who contributed heavily to this manuscript, translating, suggesting and adding valuable information, and editing the Arabic version of this book. I am also thankful to my brothers, sisters-in-law, and nephews, Sanad and Qais, who are fond of molokhia, as well as my friends in the UK, Jordan, the USA, and the UAE, for their encouragement and support throughout this interesting writing process. Special thanks to Samer Hattar for his invaluable notes.

Once again, completion of this book would not have been possible without the efforts of Karen Hall, who not only edited my manuscript meticulously, but also raised sharp questions and shared valuable insights which influenced the final book shape.

---

[1] Fairouz Taha Doleh has had a distinguished career in education spanning over 40 years, serving in various roles such as teacher, headteacher, and consultant. Her dedication to the field of education has significantly impacted the lives of many students and educators. Fairouz holds a BA in History and advanced education certificates, which have provided her with a strong foundation and expertise in her field.
After retiring, she continues to lead an active and fulfilling life. She is an avid reader and enjoys spending her time immersed in books, gardening, and cherishing moments with her grandchildren. She also contributes to her community by serving as a board member of several charities, demonstrating her commitment to giving back and helping others. She lives in Amman, Jordan, where she continues to inspire those around her with her wisdom and compassion.

About the Author

Basel Nashat Asmar is an expert in oil and gas fundamentals, costs, and technology, as well as a dynamic simulation expert with extensive computer, modelling, and simulation skills. He is currently a Director with S&P Global, based in London, UK. Dr. Asmar has previously held roles with major engineering companies involved in large liquefied natural gas (LNG) regasification and liquefaction terminals, natural gas compression stations, and offshore oil and gas production platforms. As a senior process engineer and dynamic simulation specialist, he has worked with CB&I (currently McDermott), Mott MacDonald, and IMEG, and as a lead consultant with 2050 Consulting Ltd and Trident Consultants Ltd. His academic background includes a position as a research associate at the University of Nottingham.

Basel Asmar

Besides his extensive professional experience, Dr. Asmar is also an accomplished author with four books to his name and over 50 articles published in international journals, conference proceedings, newspapers, and electronic media. He has also authored more than 60 technical reports. Dr. Asmar is a Chartered Engineer, a member of the Institution of Chemical Engineers (IChemE), a senior member of the American Institute of Chemical Engineers (AIChE), and a member of the Jordanian Engineers Association.

Despite his deep expertise in engineering and technology, Dr. Asmar also has a passion for writing on diverse subjects such as politics, history, and food, showcasing his versatility and broad intellectual interests. He holds a BSc in Chemical Engineering from the University of Jordan, an MSc in Process and Project Engineering, and a PhD in Chemical Engineering from the University of Nottingham, as well as a doctorate in Geoscience from Freie Universität Berlin, Germany.

Introduction

Molokhia, or jute leaf, are two of the over one hundred names given to this unique leafy vegetable, dubbed recently as a 'superfood'.[2] In this book I decided to spotlight a culinary treasure which, although very popular in many parts of the world, remains obscure in the West.

It is highly appreciated in the Levant and North Africa. Kids are given a taste as toddlers, most get to love it and become, dare I say, addicted. Although for some, the slimy texture of the cooked vegetable can perhaps be off-putting, making it an acquired taste, believe me, once one acquires it, one will never lose it.

molokhia fridge magnet

Until recently, those of us growing up in the Middle East, were mistakenly convinced that this vegetable was 'ours'. Imagine my surprise when, invited to a Nigerian household for a meal, I encountered this familiar vegetable, where the host passionately claimed it as 'their' traditional food! This prompted my research and opened my eyes to the fact that molokhia is a widespread staple food with footprints in most corners of the

molokhia t-shirt

[2] https://www.bbc.com/travel/article/20210802-a-superfood-fit-for-a-pharaoh

world. Interestingly, each group believes that it is uniquely their own, often unaware that many other nations use and enjoy it. In my opinion, this is because the plant names are very different between countries, thus most people do not realise they are referring to the same vegetable when describing their local cuisines.

I made the conscious choice not to write the obvious, traditional recipe book, but rather a brief guide praising and recommending this wonderful vegetable to my friends in the West.

Again, this is not intended to be a cookbook. Instead, I will take you on a journey with this beloved molokhia plant, that Levantine people consider their own, a vegetable that is seen as a jewel of their cuisine and ranked at the top of their gastronomic lists. I will explore whether this ingredient is truly exclusively Middle Eastern and North African, or if the people in the MENA region are simply unaware that other cultures cherish this ingredient also.

At the moment, the cookbook market is thriving, despite the explosion of digital media. Millions of hours of recipe demonstrations are constantly being uploaded, alongside new apps, with countless variations for every type of recipe, are evolving fast.

With this abundance of food

information, there are millions of recipes available to all to read or watch over the internet on YouTube or Cookpad for example. The once distinct borders between cuisines are blurring, with many ingredients being used in new and creative ways. Many chefs and creative individuals are experimenting with adventurous combinations. Some new recipes have gained international popularity. My wish is that molokhia will be an important part of this food evolution.

The book is divided into two parts, - 'Part I: Getting Acquainted', which introduces molokhia as a leafy vegetable in a simple high-level form; 'Part II: Molokhia as a Food Around the World', takes the reader on a global journey exploring why this unassuming vegetable is a staple ingredient in many cuisines.

I would like to invite people to experiment with this vegetable and try it in exciting 'new' ways. Readers can google or search online and having searched for these dishes online, I know they will find plenty of recipes to choose from.

Part I

Getting Acquainted

Molokhia 101

Molokhia, or jute mallow, is a species belongs to the family Malvaceae. It's a tropical plant whose origin is still debated between Africa and Asia. There are three closely related varieties of the plant. **Scientifically**, one is called Corchorus olitorius and its closely related relatives are Corchorus capsularis and Corchorus tridens. These plants are the primary source of jute fibre, the second most important fibre source after cotton. **Botanically**, the plant is related to okra and mallow, two other important edible vegetables.

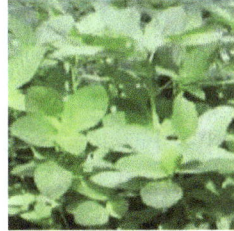

molokhia plant

The plant is tall, growing up to a height of 2–4 meters and can be either unbranched or possess a few slightly woody lateral branches. The stems and leaves of the plant can be dark green, dark red, or an intermediate colour. The leaf stalks hold shiny oval, tapered leaves with serrated edges. The plant produces yellow flowers and ridged capsules or pods (these are the fruit) that contain their seeds.

molokhia flower

The flowers, leaves, seeds and young fruits of this versatile vegetable are edible, but neither the root nor the stem can be eaten.

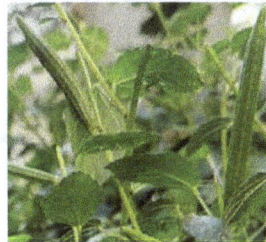

molokhia pods

As a food ingredient molokhia is mostly cooked, although it can also be eaten raw. The flavour of the leaves is mildly bitter and can taste a little grassy. The young leaves and stem tops are eaten cooked. The texture is slimy unless they are fried. The leaves also quickly become mucilaginous when cooked, similar to okra. In Part II of this book, I shed light on the many ways the vegetable is eaten.

molokhia seeds

In addition to cooking, young molokhia leaves are added to salads whilst older leaves are used more as a flavouring herb. The dried leaves can be used for tea, as a soup thickener and more recently, are also taken as health supplements.

The vegetable has been eaten for thousands of years with references to its consumption found in ancient Egypt. There are several theories on the origin of its name, with some theories suggesting its root in Arabic (Mulukia) is derived from 'royal'. In my opinion, this is truly appropriate as it is seen as the queen of vegetables in many Middle Eastern households.

Nomenclature Around the World

Language is so interesting, and although it can help us to communicate, and it can also create confusion. It can be the sounds we make or words we write in unique scripts that are perfectly clear to one person and utterly incomprehensible to another. It can be simple, and it can be complex. We teach it to our children and still as adults, we will encounter familiar words that mean something other than we might have believed.

So, it is with the word molokhia, the word itself means different things to different cultures, ethnic groups, botanists and scientists. This has created something of a challenge in itself while researching this book. Below I clarify the issue and reveal what molokhia means around the world. Think of this as a language reunion where vastly different people will discover that they all have something in common - a love of this royal superfood.

In English, the leaf is known by several common names including jute mallow, jute, bush okra, wild okra, jew's mallow, tossa jute, West African sorrel, nalta jute, Arabic jute, Egyptian spinach, and Corchorus.

In Arabic molokhia (Arabic: ملوخية) has numerous romanised spellings including mulukhiyah, moloukhiyya, mloukiya, melokhia and molochia. For the remainder of this text, I will use the word molokhia when referring to the leafy vegetable. I selected this spelling after researching numerous variations of the Arabic word in Google search and this version was the clear winner in terms of number of search results.

Furthermore, the vegetable has numerous names in many languages. For broad lists of names, please consult one of these many references.[3,4,5,6,7,8,9] My research identified over 100 names used for this plant. For each name in any language, several different spellings are used. Some of the common names used are ewedu in Nigeria, Mrenda in Kenya, saluyot in the Philippines, pat shak in Bengal, moroheiya in Japan, lalo in Haiti and corète in French. The above famous names are only the tip of the iceberg, and by no means are a comprehensive list.

Availability

As a plant, molokhia is resilient crop

[3] https://mansfeld.ipk-gatersleben.de/apex/f?p=
185:46:460593146620::NO::module,mf_use,source,akzanz,
rehm,akzname,taxid:mf,,botnam,0,,Corchorus%20olitorius,
4899
[4] https://www.healthbenefitstimes.com/jute-corchorus-
olitorius-facts/
[5] https://pfaf.org/user/plant.aspx?latinname=
corchorus+olitorius
[6] https://www.foodcooking-inspiration.in/2013/12/paat-
pata-bhaja-jute-leaves.html
[7] https://pfaf.org/user/plant.aspx?latinname=
corchorus+olitorius
[8] https://www.doc-developpement-durable.org/
file/Culture/Culture-plantes-alimentaires/FICHES_
PLANTES/corete-potagere/Corchorus_olitorius_
PFAF.pdf
[9] https://ntfp.org/2016/02/jute-or-saluyot/

and is found in many areas around the world. It grows in most areas of Africa, the Middle East, South Asia, East Asia, Southeast Asia, South America and the Caribbean.

In India, Bangladesh, the Philippines and Egypt, where molokhia leaves are consumed in large quantities as food, they are often sold in bundles in traditional markets. In many rural areas, especially in Sub-Saharan Africa, the plant grows wild, and people can harvest or forage it directly from the wild.

molokhia bunch

Nowadays, in urban areas of regions of consumption, fresh molokhia is often bought from grocery stores, supermarkets or even from the back of trucks, by roadside in its fresh form, either as full stems/bunches or as plucked leaves alone. More recently, packaged molokhia leaves, whole or chopped, frozen or dried, are available in grocery stores, supermarkets and markets.

frozen molokhia

In the US, the UK, the EU, Australia and other countries, where it is not traditionally used, the vegetable is still uncommon but is available in frozen or dried forms, in ethnic shops or supermarkets. In its frozen or dried forms, it may be labelled with the Arabic name, jute leaves or one of its African names (e.g. ewedu, muera), Filipino name (saluyot) or Haitian name (lalo).

powdered molokhia

It can also be found canned in brine (see Amazon) or even, rarely, fresh.

Recently, the processed molokhia market has increased its reach and can be bought as:

1. Microwaveable ready meals in Egypt, Jordan, or in the UK (in the Levantine recipe soup).

microwaveable molokhia ready meals

2. Ready-to-eat in jars.

ready-to-eat molokhia

3. As a baby food product.

baby food molokhia

It has also become available in the form of tea bags, coffee substitute and cocoa drink. For example, in Germany, molokhia tea is available!

molokhia tea

molokhia coffee

molokhia cocoa

Also, as a food supplement, in tablet form.

molokhia supplement tablets

Nutritional Benefits

Molokhia leaves are low in calories, contain little fat but are rich in protein and fibre. They are loaded with vitamins including Vitamins A, C and E, plus the minerals iron, calcium, phosphorus, potassium and others. It also provides beta-carotene, and is a good source of thiamine, riboflavin and ascorbic acid.

Numerous reports detail the exact contents of the leaves, alone or in certain recipes. Interested readers can consult many references.[10],[11],[12]

Medicinal Benefits

Molokhia leaves have proven nutrient qualities, as it is filled with vitamins, minerals and antioxidants that are beneficial to the body.

There are many claims about the medicinal benefits of molokhia. In traditional medicine, all the different parts of the plant have been used to treat sicknesses in many parts of the world. For example, the leaves are used to treat gonorrhoea, constipation, tumours, as well as aches and pains. However, discussing its medical benefits is outside the scope of this book, and if you want to know more, many references exist which can be consulted.

However, scanning through the

[10] https://www.nutritionix.com/i/nutritionix/molokhia-1-cup/580e6432b363847822738684
[11] https://fdc.nal.usda.gov/fdc-app.html#/food-details/168419/nutrients
[12] https://www.medindia.net/nutrition-data/jute-potherb-raw.htm

literature, there are many examples of people 'feeling good' following consumption of molokhia. Some of the benefits mentioned include its ability to act as an anti-inflammatory, it has anti-aging and immune boosting effects, improves digestion, helps easing of breathing issues like asthma, it aids with weight loss, insomnia, it improves the health of the teeth and gums, and last but not least, preserves bone density.

I am not assessing these claims here as this is outside the scope of this book, but it is fascinating to discover its other beneficial properties.

Other Uses

Besides its culinary uses, the whole plant is also used as animal fodder.

However, all these food uses are minor compared to its use as industrial crop, i.e. as a source of fibre. The stem is the main source of jute used in sack cloth, paper etc. The wood is very light and soft and is used in making sulphur matches.

drying jute fibre

jute bag

Another non-food application is its use in making soap, shower gel and skin cream products.

molokhia skin products

We are not discussing these uses here as they are outside the scope of this book.

Part II

Molokhia as Food Around the World

Due to its nature, in most cases molokhia leaf is almost exclusively being cooked in stews or soups and is rarely eaten raw. However, in this new era of 'fusion cuisine', creative usage is increasingly seeing the vegetable being experimented with.

Traditional recipes are found in many parts of the world - from Middle East to Sub-Saharan Africa, also in South Asia, Southeast Asia, East Asia and some Caribbean Islands. Its usage elsewhere is mainly confined to various diaspora communities found in Latin America, Europe and North America.

Throughout the book I use the phrase 'traditional dishes or recipes' as a way to distinguish recipes cooked for generations, from the new methods being invented these days. Note that, when we are talking about food, the concept of 'authenticity' is often controversial, and it is not an argument I am getting into in this book. (Refer to the Economist Article April 2nd 2022 p76).[13]

---

[13] https://www.economist.com/culture/2022/04/02/in-praise-of-mass-market-american-tacos

Middle Eastern and North African (Arab World) Cuisine

Molokhia is one of the most loved foods in the Middle East and North Africa. Parents introduce their kids to the dish at very young age and, I can say with confidence, that the majority love it.

Molokhia has been cooked in the region for thousands of years and the way it is cooked has hardly changed. Traditionally prepared recipes do not include ingredients from the New World, although modern variations may contain some.

While there are many techniques of how the leafy vegetable is cooked, three main variations exist. They differ by the way the vegetable is used, and each dominates in their geographic region. The three main methods are:

1. Using finely chopped leaves. It is the form used in Egypt, Sudan, Southern Levant and the Arab Peninsula.

2. Using whole leaves, either unchopped or coarsely chopped leaves. This is the form cooked in Northern Levant.

3. Using dried powdered leaves, this is cooked in Tunisia, Algeria, Libya and Mauritania.

Note that the leafy vegetable is uncommon in Morocco or Western Algeria, where the word molokhia refers to okra.

I will start by briefly describing some traditional dishes in the region, which indeed have evolved with time and with the advancement of cooking methods. I will then present new recipes, some of which have been repeated several times on the internet – an indication that they are being slowly adopted as the preferred new ways of cooking

Interestingly, the Druze, a small religious sect found mostly in Syria, Lebanon and Israel, believe in a different bodily consequence — they are forbidden to eat molokhia because it is thought to be an aphrodisiac. Who knows how this belief may contribute to its popularity in the future?

Finely Minced Molokhia (Molokhia Na'emah)

This literally means finely chopped molokhia. This dish is considered a crown jewel dish in the cuisines of Jordan and Palestine, as well as being one of the three national dishes of Egypt.[14] The dish is basically a soup based on a meat, poultry,[15] fish or shellfish broth.[16] A vegetarian version can be cooked and is popular when fasting in Lent.

molokhia na'emah

The dish is prepared in two steps, with step one comprising firstly of preparing a broth[17] from the meat (often lamb,

---

14 The other two are Kushari (made of a mixture of rice, macaroni, and lentils topped with crispy fried onions and spiced tomato sauce with garlic and vinegar) and Ful Medames (made of cooked fava beans and served with olive oil, cumin, and optionally with chopped parsley, garlic, onion, lemon juice, chilli pepper, and spices).

15 Although technically meat is animal flesh that is eaten as food. In the Middle Eastern popular terminology, meat includes all red meats from animal sources, although the only ones commonly available are beef, veal, pork, and lamb (or mutton in some countries). Poultry is the inclusive term for chicken, turkey, goose, duck, and pigeon as well as pheasants and other less available fowl. https://www.pearsonhighered.com/assets/samplechapter /0/1/3/4/0134204581.pdf

16 Many use stock and broth interchangeably, but broth is thinner than stock. Stock tends to be made more from bony parts of the meat, poultry or seafood, whereas broth is made more out of the flesh. Stock usually has a fuller mouth feel and richer flavour, due to the gelatine released by long-simmering bones.

17 Even though most use broth and stock interchangeably, there are some technical differences: the stock cooks for a long period of time (over 6 hours), and often includes bones and thus will jellify once cold. The broth is lighter, cooks with meat for a shorter period of time (1 to 2 hours depending on the recipe) and stays liquid once cold.

beef or rabbit), poultry (often chicken or pigeon), shrimp or fish (often Egyptian mackerel, Schall, sea bream, tilapia, grey mullet, or even tuna). Pieces of diced meat or chicken or fish or cleaned shrimps, are simmered in water and flavoured with spices including mistka, cardamon, cinnamon, allspice, black pepper, along with bicarbonate, etc., (depending on the type of meat poultry or fish or the regional variation). The meat, poultry or fish (but not the shrimps) are removed from the broth, which is reserved and set aside to be used for step two. The cooking of the set-aside meat, poultry or fish is then finalised as desired, with many variations used such as grilling, browning, shredding, then flavoured with garlic. In others, it can be added to the soup at the latter stages of cooking.

Step two commences once the broth is ready. It is brought to the boil, salt and pepper are added to taste, with optional bay leaves, chopped onion, tomato paste or lemon juice and, sometimes, a tomato is added, cut in half or chopped. This reduces the sliminess, and all are gently simmered. Then the finely chopped molokhia leaves are added to the broth. If fresh molokhia leaves are used, they are chopped using a special utensil (molokhia knife) or a food processor (only 2 or 3 rounds so as not to smash and make it gooey).

molokhia knife

If chopped frozen leaves are used, they are added directly to the broth without defrosting. If dried chopped leaves are used, chopped chard, spinach or mallow, as additional ingredients, are added, with the molokhia. An optional cube stock/bouillon[18] can be added along with a smashed garlic, then let the ingredients simmer till done. (Note, covering molokhia right after making it, might make it separate.) In a separate pan, chopped garlic, coriander (chopped fresh or dried), salt to taste and sometimes cumin seeds are sautéed in oil or ghee, then poured over the surface of the simmering molokhia. This is mixed together, or drizzled on top of the molokhia, before serving. The unique sound made by this addition, called tasha or qadha, is cherished. The meat, poultry or fish can be added and mixed briefly before serving. Finally lemon juice is squeezed on the top or served alongside to taste.

This dish can be served with white rice, vermicelli rice or flat bread. It can be accompanied with lemon juice, fried bread, vinegar and chopped onion sauce. If not added to the mix, meat, poultry or fish are served as side dishes accompanying the molokhia dish.

Variations include sautéing chopped coriander and garlic, adding the broth

---

[18] Bouillon is often used interchangeably with broth. The term also refers to the condensed-cube and powder forms of broth, used to add flavour to some recipes.

to them at the start, omitting the tomatoes and the tomato paste, especially from the Levantine version.

In the Hijazi or Yemeni version, the chicken and/or the meat are not removed from the broth, instead, the molokhia is added to the broth and the method is continued as above.

Also, rather than preparing the broth from scratch, meat or chicken stock cubes can be used for convenience, or using a vegetable stock cube for a vegetarian version without meat stock. And for preparing the broth and the final topping, margarine, butter, or any other shortening can be used as desired. Note that some connoisseurs have strong opinions regarding the use of coriander as an ingredient and many individual recipes omit it totally.

In some variations both meat and chicken can be used together. Also in recent recipes, chefs are experimenting with using mincemeat instead of diced meat; others are trying kufta[19] or meat balls, some are also adding liver and chicken gizzards or using smoked duck. Others have added chilli for spicier versions.

Another recent variation is in the way of

---

[19] Consist of minced meat, usually lamb or mutton, beef, chicken, (rarely pork), , or a mixture, which is mixed with spices, herbs and sometimes other ingredients. It is shaped into meatballs, discs or spread flat on trays to be baked.

serving, that is, where the toasted bread, rice and molokhia are layered then served in the form of fatta or fatteh,[20] which is very popular serving method in the Middle East and North Africa.

Whole Leaves Molokhia Stew (Molokhia Waraq)

The traditional Lebanese and Syrian recipe for molokhia is a stew that uses whole leaf molokhia, instead of the finely chopped leaves used in Egypt and Southern Levant. It comprises of molokhia leaves and meat or poultry with spices.

molokhia waraq

The preparation of the dish is simpler than the finely chopped version. It also involves two steps. Firstly, the broth preparation is similar to the method outlined in that of finely chopped molokhia, but traditionally, chicken, diced lamb or a combination of both is used. In the same pot, chopped coriander, whole garlic and chopped onion are sautéed in olive oil. Then, either washed whole leaves or coarsely chopped molokhia, are added in batches with allspice, salt to taste, along with other spices, as desired, sautéed and stirred until well combined. The preferred broth is added and allowed to

---

[20] Fatteh is an Egyptian, Levantine or Iraqi dish consisting of pieces of fresh, toasted, grilled, or fried flatbread covered with other ingredients that vary according to region.

thicken. When the molokhia softens, the set-aside chicken or meat is added. Finally, lemon juice or lemon slices are added, and everything is simmered.

The dish is served with rice or flat bread, accompanied with chopped onion in vinegar or lemon juice as a side dish.

In some variations, both meat and chicken are used together. Purified butter, vegetable oil or other shortening can be used. One can also prepare a vegetarian version using vegetable broth or a vegetable bouillon cube. This dish is popular during Lent fasting. Sometimes roasted onion is sprinkled on top before serving.

Again, recently, some cooks have experimented with using mincemeat instead of diced meat. Some add chilli for spicier versions. Vegetarians can substitute meat and chicken with shredded jackfruit.

Stir Fried Molokhia (bi Zeit)

This is a light stir-fried version of molokhia, often cooked as a fasting version at Lent.

molokhia bi zeit

The preparation of the dish is simple. Start by getting the diced onions, chopped garlic and optional chilli sautéed in olive oil. Stir in coriander powder with salt and black pepper to taste. Coarsely chopped or whole molokhia leaves are then added in batches and cooked, stirring frequently. The molokhia is ready when it turns darker, and the liquid has been absorbed. Once removed from heat, lemon juice is added and is mixed-in well.

It can be served hot or cold, often with flat bread and sometimes with plain rice.

Variations can include using different types of vegetable oils, adding chopped tomatoes, chilli paste, adding stir-fried garlic and coriander on top, or adding pomegranate molasses.

Shalawlaw/Shalaolao

A simple Sa'idi[21] or Upper Egyptian recipe popular with the Copts, especially during fasting in Lent. It gained some notoriety in the media after an Egyptian politician claimed that it is a cure for the Covid-19 virus.

shalawlaw

It is made of dried and ground molokhia leaves in cold water with lots of garlic and lemon juice. Minced garlic, salt, green and red chilli, and if desired, cumin and dried coriander are mixed

---

[21] Al-Sa'id (الصعيد) is the name given to Upper Egypt south of Cairo.

together. The lemon juice and the dried molokhia are added and all are mixed together. Cold water is added gradually and whisked to reach desired consistency. Note, the water needs to be chilled and sometimes ice is added if the water is not cold enough. It is topped with leftover lemon peel and shatta[22] (if desired).

The dish is served cold with flat bread, accompanied with raw onion or spring onion. Variations include adding chopped tomatoes, or using cold broth instead of cold water.

A related dish is popular in Damietta, called Damietta salad. Here the recipe is similar to shalawlaw, but additional vegetables can be added including diced tomatoes, cucumber, green pepper, diced onion, green or black olives, fresh mint and other spices, such as ground white pepper or dried mint.

Bissara

Bissara is a North African and Levantine dip and/or thick soup, often made of dried fava beans and sometimes dried molokhia, especially in the Southern Levant.

bissara

The dish preparation is simple. Dried

---

[22] Shatta is a spicy sauce made of red chillies, lemon juice, garlic, and chilli powder.

fava beans are boiled in water until the fava beans soften and starts creating a paste. Optionally, one can sauté chopped onion in olive oil and then add it to the mix. Dried powdered molokhia leaves are then added, mixed and simmered. Chopped garlic, dried and/or fresh chopped coriander, chilli, salt (to taste) are added. Other spices, such as cumin, cayenne pepper, are sautéed in olive oil, then mixed with the paste. It is garnished with oil, red chilli, mint and fried sliced onion.

The dish is served either hot or cold, with bread, olive oil and lots of lemon juice.

Alternative versions use dried chickpea, dried lentil or dried green peas, with, or instead of fava beans. Sometimes coriander is omitted, whereas in some Egyptian variations, molokhia is substituted with dill, coriander and mint.

Note that, in Tunisia, Algeria and Morocco, the dish is cooked without molokhia but still has the same name! It is a popular street food but has different consistency and is served as soup.

Tunisian Molokhia

The name molokhia refers to two different vegetables in the Maghreb region of North Africa. While it refers to the molokhia leafy vegetable in Tunisia, Libya, Eastern and Southern Algeria, it refers to okra in Morocco and Western Algeria, where the other leafy vegetable is not eaten.

Tunisian molokhia

The preparation of the dish takes a long time, exceeding eight hours and, in many instances, it is cooked overnight. It has two main steps. First, the diced meat, often beef, lamb or chicken, is marinated with spices including tabil[23] or ras hanout,[24] caraway, harissa, tomato paste, ground pepper, ground pasted garlic and salt to taste. This can be done a day before. In a separate pot the dried molokhia powder is mixed with olive oil, add the bay leaves and water; bring to boil and return to a simmer. The molokhia is brought to a boil, the meat is then added, and the mix is simmered again. When the oil rises to the top, it means the stew is ready.

This dish is often served with a fresh baguette or Italian bread (khobz Talian).

Variations include the adding of

---

[23] Tabil is a Tunisian spice blend contains all or some of coriander seeds, caraway seeds, fennel seeds, chilli powder, black peppercorns, cumin seeds, round cloves (powder), and turmeric powder.

[24] Ras haunt is a spice mixture usually consists of over a dozen spices, in different proportions. Commonly used ingredients include cardamom, cumin, clove, cinnamon, nutmeg, mace, allspice, dry ginger, chilli peppers, coriander seed, peppercorn, sweet and hot paprika, fenugreek, and dry turmeric.

powdered dried mint, powdered dried orange peel, or even dried and pounded pomegranate peel, which gives a bitter aftertaste or, using other vegetable oils and/or adding chopped onion. Other local types of meat can be used, such as rabbit, camel, pieces of tripe or merguez, a type of North African sausage.

Mauritanian Couscous (Ngomou or Hakko)

Couscous is a traditional North African ingredient made of semolina and is considered a staple food in the Maghreb Region. In Mauritania, it is made distinctive by using molokhia powder.

Mauritanian couscous

The preparation of this dish is another complex, time-intensive process. It is prepared in several main stages. First, the lamb pieces are simmered in water with chopped garlic and onions, spices, including cumin, coriander, black pepper and salt to taste. Various whole peeled fruit and vegetables are added, including carrots, potatoes, tomatoes, leeks and prunes. Once tender they are drained, removed and set aside, with the broth retained.

The second stage involves cooking the couscous by steaming it in the couscoussière (type of steamer).

couscoussière

Thirdly, diced peppers, parsley,

coriander and raisins are mixed with olives in a separate bowl to make a flavouring sauce. The sauce is mixed into the couscous, then all the ingredients are steamed again in the couscoussière. The mixture is emptied into a bowl, combined with powdered dried molokhia (called takkya or lallo in Mauritania) and the resultant combination is steamed in the couscoussière for a third time.

Fourthly, the steamed couscous is mixed with the meat prepared earlier, along with the vegetable broth and cooked further.
Finally, the couscous is placed on a plate then topped with the meat and vegetables.

This couscous is served as a main, complete, dish.

Numerous variations exist, using chicken, beef or fish instead of lamb, or using dried meat, offal or merguez (Mauritanian or Moroccan sausage). Other vegetable options such as turnips, cabbage or beans can be substituted too. It can also be dressed with milk or butter.

Sudanese Molokhia Stew

Sudanese molokhia

This is a popular dish eaten in Sudan and South Sudan. It is often called Kudra Mafrook and has similarities to the Egyptian version of the dish. It consists of minced molokhia leaves, meat or chicken and spices. In Egyptian cooking, molokhia leaves are traditionally finely chopped, but in Sudan they are blended into a paste instead.

The preparation of the dish is straightforward. Begin by boiling the meat (chicken, lamb or beef), diced onions and powdered coriander in water; bicarbonate soda is added, and the meat is removed or set-aside. The molokhia leaves are added, along with more bicarbonate soda. There are two ways to add the leaves. Either minced before adding to the soup, or adding the leaves whole, then blending, using a special utensil called a Mifrak or Lofrega (a special wooden ladle). Ice cubes, minced garlic, optional dill and salt to taste are also added. If using frozen molokhia leaves, defrost thoroughly before adding to the soup. Continue to stir the mixture until tender.

mifrak

It is often served with kisra (which is a type of sourdough pancake made from fermented and slightly acidic millet flour), or Injera,[25] and sometimes white rice. Occasionally, the set-aside meat can also be added to the soup before serving.

---

[25] Injera is a sour fermented pancake-like flatbread with a slightly spongy texture, traditionally made of teff flour. In Ethiopia and Eritrea.

Variations of the dish include the addition of extra spices such as black pepper; using lamb or beef cuts, including bones, such as oxtail or lamb shank; or using other vegetable oils and adding chicken or meat bouillon cubes. In the vegetarian version, omit the meat or chicken, instead perhaps using black-eyed peas and using vegetable stock, or add a bouillon cube.

Middle Eastern Creative Experimentation

food experimentation is increasing in the Middle East. There is an interesting trend using unconventional, unusual, or rare ingredients in traditional recipes and dishes. Since molokhia leaves are one of the most popular ingredients in traditional dishes, we are seeing many examples where it is being used in new ways.

Most of the following products use fresh molokhia leaves as an ingredient:

1. Molokhia fatayer or open pastries, with only molokhia as the topping or with spinach and feta.

molokhia open pastries

2. Molokhia as a pizza topping.

molokhia pizza

3. Molokhia and fava bean stew, uniting the two main dishes of Egypt.

molokhia and fava bean stew

4. Stuffed molokhia leaves.

preparation of stuffed molokhia leaves

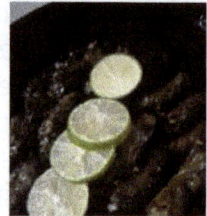

stuffed molokhia leaves

5. Molokhia juice – several types - on its own, with other vegetables, as an energy drink. Even a play on the word 'mocktail' with the name 'mokhito' instead of mojito!

molokhia juice

6. Surprisingly, I did not find any recipes for molokhia tabbouleh or fatayer, similar to spinach fatayer. A potential gap in the market maybe?

molokhia fatayer

Other Middle Eastern or Mediterranean Cuisines

Surprisingly, unlike other stars of Middle Eastern cuisine, namely aubergine (eggplant), chickpea (garbanzo bean), fava bean (broad bean) or okra (ladies' fingers), molokhia did not make the leap into other Middle Eastern cuisines, with a few exceptions. It is not a traditionally found in Persian, Kurdish, Turkish cuisines or that of the Caucasus. The exception is Cyprus.

In Cyprus, molokhia is cooked all over the island. It is thought that the recipes used on the island were influenced by the Levantine and Egyptian cuisines. References mention that it was once popular in Crete, but this does not appear to be the case at the moment.

Cypriot Molokhia Stew (Molohiya)

This dish appears to have come to the island from Egypt and is based on the Egyptian minced molokhia recipe, adapted slightly. It is popular with the Turkish Cypriot communities, but also has crossed the North/South border of Cyprus and is now eaten everywhere.

Cypriot molokhia stew (molohiya)

The dish is prepared in two steps. First, chicken pieces are fried in oil and set aside. Chopped onion and sliced garlic are sautéed in oil, then the chicken is added, followed by chopped tomatoes, tomato paste, optional pepper paste, chicken stock, salt and ground black pepper to taste. These are all mixed together, then the drained molokhia leaves are added to the pan, followed by lemon juice. All are stirred well and brought to boil, then simmered for a while. The chicken is added, along with more lemon juice and all is simmered until cooked. Note that for this dish, molokhia leaves are first dried in the sun, then the leaves are pre-boiled in lemon juice, before adding in for the cooking process.

The dish can be served with rice or Cypriot seeded bread.

Variations of the dish can use lamb instead of chicken. The vegetarian option uses no meat or meat stock, instead, adding potatoes into the broth.

Sub-Saharan African Cuisine

Despite being thought to have originated in Ethiopia, molokhia is not traditionally eaten there. However, in Sub-Saharan Africa, the use of molokhia in local cooking is widespread. Sub-Saharan Africa has four main regions: Western Africa, Central or Middle Africa, Eastern Africa and Southern Africa.[26] In each of these regions, the use of molokhia varies between ethnic groups, even in the same countries. It has been named one of the top ten most popular vegetables in Africa.[27]

The plant is cultivated throughout Sub-Saharan Africa, although in many cases the cultivation is not commercial and, in many regions, the plant grows in the wild.

In Western Africa, molokhia is commonly eaten across the whole region and the leafy vegetable is known by several local names. Throughout the region, the vegetable is a main ingredient in many soups and stews. Although one finds many recipes with various names, in essence, most people

---

[26] The definition of each region varies and differs between international organisations.
[27] https://foodeely.com/10-popular-vegetables-in-africa/

in West Africa cook molokhia is comparable ways and the variations are tweaks rather than fundamentally different cooking processes.

In the Central or Middle Africa region, the spread of the vegetable is lower than Western Africa, but it is still very common with some communities in counties such as Cameroon, Congo and Chad.

In Eastern Africa, alleged home of the plant, the vegetable is used by some ethnic groups in Kenya, Uganda and South Sudan. It is used to a lesser extent in other parts of the region.

In Southern Africa, it appears that the plant has yet to be cultivated commercially. Despite this, its use is widespread, it carries local names and is used by many ethnic groups. It has not gained the prominence seen in Western or Northern Africa. It is considered more of a minor food ingredient. It is eaten either raw or cooked. Seeds and younger leaves are added to salads or cooked, while older leaves may be used to make tea. It is mainly used to thicken soups.

In this region the names of molokhia and okra are mixed in many languages and dialects, therefore when searching on the internet, okra appears in the search instead of molokhia in many instances. The reason for this appears to be that the words may relate to the glutinous or mucilaginous nature of the two related vegetables. In many Southern African languages molokhia is referred to as wild okra and many consider molokhia to be a wild weed cousin of okra.

Some of the most common traditional dishes are described below. They represent the most popular types of dishes so I will avoid using local names as this may cause confusion. This is not an exhaustive list of all the ways molokhia is cooked in the region. I am in no-way trying to ignore ethnicities by omitting their dishes, but I found that in many cases, very similar recipes have different names and indeed each group is proud of its own version. As I said earlier, some creative recipes are emerging, with many diaspora Africans experimenting with new ways of cooking molokhia, creating fusion dishes and adapting to its availability in their location, e.g. often using the frozen version, as it is more readily available in the West.

One interesting fact to note that in Sub-Saharan Africa they prefer the gooey nature of the consistency of the dish – in fact it is desirable to have the dish in the form of a slimy sauce, very similar to that of okra pods. This is in contrast to the attitude in the Middle East, where they try to reduce the sliminess as much as they can, and consider the slimy consistency of the dish to be highly undesirable.

West African Molokhia Soup

Molokhia soup is a rich, lush, dark green, mucilaginous soup, popular across all of West Africa. It consists of molokhia leaves and spices. It is known by many names, including Ewedu soup, ayoyo soup, ademe soup, to list just a few. To get an idea of the many other names, consult the nomenclature section earlier in the book. It is widely eaten in most West African countries including Nigeria, Togo, Benin, Ghana, Cote d'Ivoire, Burkina Faso and Cameroon. It is often called 'Draw Soup', due to the mucilaginous nature that gives it a slippery and viscous texture.

West African molokhia soup

The preparation differs depending on if one is using fresh or frozen leaves. If fresh leaves are used, they are boiled in water, then mashed using a special short broom known in Yoruba as ijabe (practically a whisk) till they are fully blended and look quite slimy. If you do not have an ijabe in your kitchen, a blender or food processor can be used instead. If frozen leaves are used, they are thawed then blended until smooth in a hand blender or food processor and brought to the boil in water. Then additional ingredients are spices are added including ground crayfish, bouillon and the spices - cayenne

ijabe

45

pepper, salt to taste and iru.[28] They are stirred and simmered for few minutes.

It is often served with fufu or other swallow types[29] made of cassava, yam, plantain, etc., a bean sauce and a stew of fish or meat.

There are many variations to the dish, which are in fact different recipes, but I have grouped them together here as the preparation processes are so similar, e.g. adding egusi[30] powder or peanut paste to thicken the soup, or adding kaun.[31] Also the vegetables can be cooked in meat stock instead of water.

West African Molokhia Stew

This stew or soup is quite similar to the soup described earlier, but it is distinctive by the addition of meat or fish directly, throughout the cooking process. It is also popular in West Africa, particularly in Benin, Cote d'Ivoire and Ghana. It has many local names including crincrin, ademe, ayoyo, kplala, kolala, nanounkoun, nin-nouwi and kèlèn-kèlèn.

West African molokhia stew

---

[28] Iru is fermented locust beans
[29] Sticky dough that consists of a starchy rot vegetable compacted by hand into small balls. usually swallowed without chewing.
[30] Egusi is ground African melon seeds.
[31] Kaun is a general name for minerals or inorganic compounds that contain potassium used in small quantities in West African cooking sometimes.

The preparation process starts by boiling beef skin, crabs, smoked fish, garlic paste, ginger paste, locust bean powder, adding salt to taste, cooking and then setting aside. Bring the chopped molokhia leaves (or frozen version) to the boil with baking soda and stir vigorously. The mix of spiced beef skin, crab and fish are combined together with the molokhia, alongside scotch bonnet or habanero and simmered until it is tender.

It is often served with fufu or other vegetable types - cassava, yam, plantain, etc, and rich tomato stew.

There are many variations to this dish and, for many of the passionately interested parties, they are considered to be totally different recipes. In reality, although each recipe is actually prepared in a different manner and has a distinct taste, since the preparation methods are quite similar, for convenience, I am keeping them here together. Amongst the variations are: omitting the beef skin or any meat; adding other seafood varieties; using chicken; using additional or alternative spices, such as calabash, nutmeg or lanhoin (aged salted fish); adding ground seeds such as pumpkin seeds; roasted peanuts and adding other vegetables such as okra.

West African Molokhia Stew/Soup with Palm Oil

This soup is similar to the West African soup described earlier, but it is distinctive by the addition of substantial amounts of palm oil and incorporating meat or fish directly, throughout the cooking process. It too is popular in West Africa, particularly in Sierra Leone, Liberia, Cote d'Ivoire, etc. It has many local names including plasas sauce, palaver sauce, Kren-kren,[32] ademe, ayoyo, kplala, kolala, nanounkoun , and nin-nouwi.

West African molokhia stew/soup with palm oil

The preparation is quite involved and has two separate steps. The first step is the preparation of the assorted meats which can include lamb, beef, goat or seafood. The second step is the combining of the ingredients together. The process starts by simmering the meat and simmering chopped onion, chopped tomatoes, tomato paste, garlic, ginger, chilli pepper, scotch bonnet pepper or habanero. The palm oil is stirred in, followed by a bouillon cube or traditional spices. These can include fermented sesame seeds or fermented, roasted, locust beans, dried anchovies, crayfish or fish powder etc. Then add the molokhia leaves, salt to taste, followed by adding the prepared fish, red palm oil and simmering until tender.

---

[32] Also spelled krain krain or crain crain

It is often served with rice or with fufu or other swallow types made of cassava, yam, plantain, etc., and bean sauce, and a stew of fish or meat.

There are many variations to this dish, and again, for many of the various experts, they are considered entirely different recipes. Although each recipe is actually prepared in a distinct manner and has a unique taste, as the preparation methods are quite similar, I am grouping them together here for convenience. Amongst the variations are the use of coconut oil or peanut oil as substitutes to palm oil; adding ground agushi (white melon seeds) or other ground seeds; or adding crab or other seafood varieties; or adding other vegetables such as chopped okra.

Dried Molokhia Stew - Mali

This dish is popular in Northern Mali, Chad, Niger, and uses dried molokhia leaves instead of fresh leaves. It is locally called fakoye. It has some similarities with Tunisian molokhia.

dried molokhia stew - Mali

The dish is prepared by adding diced mutton to oil or shea butter, with salt to taste, chopped onion, tomatoes, powdered and chopped garlic. Spices include fermented locust beans powder (often called soumbala or dawadawa), black pepper, paprika, aniseed, dried fish powder, all-purpose seasoning or bouillon, and date or tamarind molasses. Then add the powdered dried molokhia leaves, chilli or scotch bonnet or habanero, and let simmer till cooked.

It is typically served with rice.

Variations include using ghee or adding other spices, including guinea pepper, dried fish or using date fruit.

Okra and Molokhia Stew (Superkanja)

This dish is popular in The Gambia, Senegal and Guinea. It traditionally uses okra as one of its main ingredients, but in many instances, molokhia is also added to the dish.

okra and molokhia stew (superkanja)

The preparation of the dish is relatively straightforward consisting of two main steps. First preparing the meat included in the recipe, then combining the whole dish together. The meat and dried fish are boiled, then the fish is placed to the side. Salt, to taste, is added to the meat, along with chopped onions, pepper, diced okra, molokhia leaves, chilli powder and an optional bouillon cube. This is mixed well and cooked for a while, then palm oil is added before bringing to a simmer. Finally, the fish is returned, and the ingredients are allowed to simmer.

It is served with white rice, fufu or other types of starchy swallows.

Variations can include adding crabs and shrimps; the vegetarian option of adding spinach, collards, kale, turnip greens, okra leaves or sweet potato leaves.

Chadian Molokhia Stew

This dish is composed of beef and molokhia leaves. It is similar to the Sudanese version, but without beating the molokhia or liquidising the stock with the hand blender.

Chadian molokhia stew

The preparation of the dish is simple. First sauté the onion and garlic in peanut oil. Add the diced beef, season with salt and black pepper, then fry the mixture until it browns. The chopped fresh or frozen molokhia leaves are added, with water, baking soda and chilli powder, then simmered until tender. Simmer for 30-45 minutes, until a thick stew has formed, and the meat is tender. If needed, continue to cook uncovered until the stew reduces to a sauce.

It is served with plain rice or kissar, which is a sourdough pancake made from fermented, slightly acidic millet flour.

Variations include using different

vegetable oil or, in recent times, using other types of meat.

Greens Stew

Popular in Central African region, particularly Congo and Cameroon, where several vegetables are stewed together with palm oil or palm butter.

green stew

This is a simple dish where chopped onion is sautéed in palm oil, then shredded green leaves of cassava, kale, collards, molokhia or similar are added, as well as chopped okra, chilli, cayenne pepper or red pepper, salt to taste and cooked till tender.

It is often served with starchy swallow.

Variations include using different types of leafy vegetables or using peanut butter as a substitute to palm oil. Another variation is to prepare a meat version with diced meat added prior to the vegetables.

Southern African Molokhia Soup

Generally speaking, the molokhia soups made in the Southern African region are modest compared to their West African counterparts. They often use molokhia as one of several vegetables in a simple recipe. These dishes are eaten in most Southern African countries including Zambia, Zimbabwe, Malawi, Botswana and South Africa.

Southern African molokhia soup

The dishes go by many names including delele, derere, thelele, guxe, etc. There is name confusion when looking at English references between okra and molokhia in local languages. This is because in these languages, molokhia is known as wild okra. The two plants are related closely and share the mucilaginous (thickening) quality when cooked.

Preparing the dish is easy: start by adding salt and baking soda to boiling water, add roughly chopped molokhia leaves and stir for several minutes. In a separate pot or pan, sauté the tomatoes, chopped chilli, onions or spring onions in vegetable oil, then the molokhia leaves mixture is added, stir together until mixed and simmer until tender.

It is often served with starchy swallow such as pap or plain rice.

Variations include chopping the leaves finely to increase the sliminess; adding the chopped okra, before adding the molokhia, in the cooking process; adding other leafy vegetables such as pumpkin leaves or seeds such as melon seeds. In Eswatini (formerly known as Swaziland), the leaves are mashed while cooking, giving it a thick and somewhat slimy consistency, which is an acquired taste for some people.

East African Molokhia Soup

This dish is popular in the Western and Nyanza provinces of Kenya among many ethnic groups, such as the Luhya. In Uganda, it is popular with the Lugbara people. It is eaten in Northwestern parts, the adjacent parts in the Congo and by the Acholi people. The vegetable has several local names including mrenda, murere, likhu, omrere, pala bi, and otigo diri.

East African molokhia soup

The dish is prepared by boiling whole molokhia leaves in water, with added salt to taste and baking soda. In another pot, sauté chopped onions with chopped tomatoes, then add the boiled leaves, stir the mixture and leave to simmer. Then add milk and let it simmer. The milk is added to reduce the bitterness often associated with the leaves.

The dish is served with rice or ugali, a type of starchy swallow, similar to Italian polenta,

Variations include omitting the milk or adding cowpea leaves and other leafy vegetables to the molokhia leaves.

Stir-Fry Molokhia

Although many scholars suggest that molokhia plants origin is from Ethiopia, the leafy plant is not a popular culinary ingredient in that country. It is sometimes used in a simple stir-fry dish.

stir-fry molokhia

The preparation of the dish is simple. Whole molokhia leaves are stir-fried with vegetable oil, salt to taste. Then, in a separate pot, chopped onion is sautéed with oil, purified vegetable butter (nitter kibbeh) and berbere spice blend.[33] Then the fried molokhia leaves are added to the second pot, where all the ingredients are mixed and simmered till tender.

It is served with injera (a sour fermented flatbread with a slightly spongy texture).

A variation includes adding diced potatoes to the dish and garnishing with roasted nuts on top.

Molokhia and Lentil Stew

An Eritrean vegan dish composed of molokhia and lentils. This has

---

[33] Berbere spice blend is berbere is a traditional Ethiopian spice blend composed of chiles, garlic, fenugreek and a handful of warm spices, such as allspice and cinnamon.

similarities to Egyptian or Palestinian bissara.

The preparation starts by sautéing chopped onion in avocado oil, adding berbere powder, berbere paste, chopped garlic, salt to taste, then adding tomato puree, red lentils and a vegetable bouillon cube. Lastly, add the chopped fresh or frozen molokhia leaves and simmer it until tender.

molokhia and lentil stew

It is served with turmeric rice or injera.

Variations include using different vegetable oil; adding chilli or pepper for a spicier version; adding cumin or other spices or using green lentils.

South Asian Cuisine

The cultivation of molokhia is widespread across the entire Indian Subcontinent with the plant farmed commercially, as well as growing in the wild. In most cases the plant is used industrially for its natural fibre although it is losing market share due to the domination of synthetic fibres.

Molokhia has many names in local languages in the Indian Subcontinent. It is referred to as jute leaves (not in English but translated into local languages). For culinary use, it is used as a main ingredient in many dishes in several South Asian cuisines. It is popular in several cuisines in Bangladesh, Eastern and Northeastern states of India, in the Bengali and Assamese cuisines, as well as in Tripura and in several ethnic tribal cuisines in the Northeastern Indian states. Its popularity also spread to neighbouring Indian cuisines particularly in Bihar and Odisha.

Curiously, the vegetable is prominent in two neighbouring geographically, but distant cuisines, in terms of culinary classification. Namely the Bengali cuisine, which relates closely to other Northern Indian cuisines, influenced by historic Moghul cuisine, characterised by heavy use of spices and chilli; and the

Assamese cuisine, which is more related to Southeastern Asian cuisines, characterised by using a wide variety of local plants (vegetables and fruits), animal products and little use of spices.

In Southern India, the vegetable appears rarely as a food ingredient, while in Northwestern India, North Central India, Western India, Pakistan and Sri Lanka, it is not used in traditional dishes.

Here again, when considering molokhia, the recipes vary mainly in the ways the vegetable is used, whether whole leaves or finely chopped. The leaves are used fresh or dried and recently, also frozen.

In addition, a rare way sometimes found is in one cuisine where the flower pods are used!

What is noticeable here is the wide variation of the cooking processes and end products, when compared to previous cuisines. In the following pages I present a selection of several traditional dishes. These recipes have evolved with time, the advancement of cooking methods and some dishes continue to evolve, with numerous media channels full of new creative recipes.

Molokhia Curry

The most popular molokhia dish in the Bengal is traditionally a vegan soup dish made of molokhia leaves and spices.

molokhia curry

Its anglicised Bengali name has several spellings amongst them -pat shaker jhol and nali sag. In Assamese it is mora xaak or morapaat.

Preparing the traditional dish is quick and easy. Molokhia leaves are chopped coarsely and placed in a pot of boiling water, with chopped onion, adding salt to taste. Chopped garlic, more chopped onion, whole green chilli, dry red chilli, nigella seeds are stir-fried in mustard oil and the mix is added to the pot to simmer for a few minutes.

This dish is served with plain rice.

Variations include using vegetable oil, olive oil or coconut oil, not using the onion, adding panch phoron,[34] turmeric or poppy seeds.

In many instances a variety of pulses can be combined with the molokhia leaves, mostly lentils, to cook famous dal recipes. In these cases, lentils or

---

[34] A mixture of spices used in Bangladeshi, Eastern and Northeastern Indian cooking. Main ingredients: fenugreek seed, nigella seed, cumin seed, black mustard seed and fennel seed.

moong lentils are used. Another variation is to add jackfruit seeds. Other recipes also add coconut flakes with the lentils.

Non-vegetarian variations include adding prawns or several types of fish such as catfish and pool barb (puti) fish. In these instances, the shrimp or fish are marinated prior to being added to the mixture. Chicken can also be used in this recipe if preferred.

Another variation involves adding the garlic, chilli and finely chopped molokhia leaves to boiling water, cooking together without any oil. Although the traditional recipes are often diluted to have a soupy texture, some prefer to serve thicker, drier versions by allowing more water to evaporate.

In Andhra Pradesh in South India, a rare version uses jackfruit as a main ingredient, alongside molokhia leaves and Guntur chilli. The leaves are used to add body, producing a consistency similar to that of a starchy cornflour soup.

Molokhia Fritters

In the Indian subcontinent, fritters are

very popular and can be made from many vegetables. Molokhia fritters are popular snacks in Bangladesh, West Bengal, Assam, Odisha and adjacent areas. Several methods exist to prepare the fritters, these differ in the type of the flour used or the spices added.

a variation of molokhia fritters

The anglicised Bengali names have several spellings, amongst them pat patar bora/pakoda, and, in Assam, Mora xaak bor.

another variation of molokhia fritters

The preparation is simple and involves covering the molokhia leaves with a binder or batter. The binder or batter is made by mixing a variety of ingredients that often include one type of flour or a combination of whole wheat flour, rice flour, gram flour, optional semolina, red chilli powder, chopped green chillies, turmeric powder, salt as required and sugar, adding a little water at a time. A single leaf, or 3-4 leaves together, are dipped into the binder mix and coated well with the batter, they are then fried in batches, in mustard oil, turning constantly.

It is often served as a side dish, accompanying plain rice or dal.

Variations include using other types of oil.

In the Assamese version, a few leaves are tied together, and the knotted leaves are dipped in the mix and fried.

Stir Fried Molokhia

A simple quick dish made of spiced molokhia leaves.

A quick dish that is prepared by removing the mid-stem from the leaves then coarsely chopping them. Nigella seeds, dried red chillies and crushed garlic are stir-fried in oil (often mustard oil), then the molokhia leaves are added, followed by turmeric, slitted green chillies and salt to taste. Cook on low heat till water (from the leaves) evaporates.

stir fried molokhia

This dish is served with plain rice.

Variations include adding chopped onion and using other types of vegetable oil. Non-vegetarian versions add fish eggs, prawns or fish, which have been marinated earlier; adding other vegetables, such as potatoes or pumpkin and adding coconut paste. Some recipes add chicken.

In Assamese cuisine the dish is simpler, with less ingredients used. In this cuisine the preparation starts by tying two or three molokhia leaves with stems together and make a knot. Then garlic is stir- fried in mustard oil, followed by the knotted leaves and salt to taste, then sprinkled with khar.[35]

Molokhia Shukto

Shukto is a popular vegetable dish in Bengali cuisine It is a bitter, pungent stew of vegetables cooked in mustard oil with numerous spices, ginger paste and chillies. It can include bori (sundried lentil dumplings), many vegetables, such as bitter gourd, moringa (drumstick), plantain, green bananas, unripe papaya, aubergine/eggplant, cucumber, white radish, potato, sweet potato, green beans and Hyacinth Bean.

molokhia shukto

Shukto has numerous variations and is prepared in many different ways. The version described contains molokhia leaves.

Because it contains many ingredients, there is no definitive list and thus, the preparation process depends on the vegetables used. Basically, the vegetables are chopped and prepped in three ways where some, such as the potato, needs to be parboiled and set aside. Others, such as aubergine, will need to be either dried and set aside or fried directly. Once the vegetables are ready, stir-fry some of the spices (including panch phoron, celery seeds) mustard paste, ginger paste in mustard

---

[35] Khar is an alkali prepared from sun dried skin of some varieties of banana.

oil, then add the vegetables, including the molokhia leaves, gradually. Stir-fry all the ingredients then add remaining spices, such as turmeric or salt to taste, finally adding water and cooking until tender.

The dish is often served at feasts with plain rice.

As indicated earlier there are numerous variations to this dish, some include adding milk and gram flour to balance the bitterness; others adding grated coconut or adding fish. Also, placing ghee on the top and adding a garnish before serving.

Molokhia with Indian Cottage Cheese (Paneer)

This is a version of the saag paneer, which is spinach and Indian cheese.

The preparation is straightforward. First boil coarsely chopped molokhia leaves with chopped onion, then set aside. In a separate pan, sauté chopped onion, chopped garlic and ginger paste. Then add chopped tomato, green chilli, turmeric, chilli powder and salt, cook for few minutes, then the paneer cubes are added and stir-fried. The previously set-aside molokhia leaves are added and stirred till cooked.

molokhia with Indian cottage cheese (paneer)

This is served as a side dish with bread e.g. chapatis (a flatbread also known as roti) or naans (leavened flatbread, baked in a tandoor or oven).

Variations included pre-frying the paneer cubes before adding to the cooking process or using different vegetable oils.

Molokhia Flatbread (Paratha)

Paratha is a type of flatbread widely used in the Indian Subcontinent, as well as amongst Indian communities in the Caribbean, Southeast Asia and East Africa. It can be baked plain or stuffed with vegetables. One variety uses molokhia.

molokhia flatbread (paratha)

The preparation starts by blanching molokhia leaves, then mixing red pepper powder, cumin, coriander powder, asafoetida, crushed black pepper powder, with salt to taste, in whole wheat flour and besan/chickpea flour. The blanched molokhia leaves are then added and all mixed together, kneading it all very well with some water. It is then divided into portions, rolled into shape and baked.

It is served as type of bread.

Molokhia Flower Curry
(Sanei Ke Phool Ki Sabzi)

Sanei phool is the flower of molokhia plant and thus, this particular recipe is different as it does not use the leaves. It is adored in West Bengal, Bihar and Uttar Pradesh

uncooked molokhia flowers

The preparation is simple. Start by sautéing garlic, red chilli, mustard seed paste and fenugreek seeds in mustard oil. The flowers are added, followed by other spices, including ground masala, salt and water. All are mixed together well, covered and cooked till tender. Once the water has evaporated, the mix is mashed and then served.

It is often accompanied by bread, with some ghee over it.

molokhia flower curry (sanei ke phool ki sabzi)

Molokhia Flower Fritters

This underrated dish made of molokhia flower buds is served as a popular snack in Bihar and Uttar Pradesh.

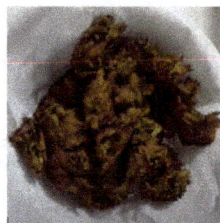

The molokhia yellow flowers, that are partially or fully bloomed, are removed as they are a little bitter, so only the buds are utilised. They are mixed with a coarse paste of garlic, green chillies, gram flour and spices (including turmeric, coriander powder, garam masala and red chilli powder). Then the

molokhia flower fritters

mixture is shaped and fried in hot mustard oil.

Variations include using other types of oil, boiling the buds before mixing them and adding chopped onion.

Boiled Molokhia

This is a very simple quick recipe eaten in North-eastern India.

boiled molokhia

Molokhia leaves and green chillies are added to water, with salt to taste, then brought to the boil. When the leaves become soft and tender, fermented bamboo shoots and mustard oil are added.

It is often served with bread or rice.

Variations include adding or using other vegetables to the mix.

Dry Molokhia Curry

A traditional dish from the Bodo cuisine of Assam in Northeastern India, is made of dried molokhia leaves and often referred to as NarziWngkri.

dry molokhia curry

The preparation of this dish is time consuming. Firstly, dried molokhia leaves are soaked, rinsed, finely chopped, then boiled with khar and water until the leaves begin to disintegrate, then they are set aside. Secondly, onion paste, and ginger-garlic paste are sautéed. Pork pieces, turmeric, cumin, slit green chilli, with salt, to taste, are added and cooked, stirring occasionally. The molokhia leaves are stirred into the mix and all are simmered until the gravy thickens.

The dish is served with hot steamed rice.

Several variations of this dish exist. The pork can be pre-boiled before use in the recipe. Fried fish can replace the pork. Also, additional spices such as garam masala, chilli or chilli powder can be added for spicier version. Vegetarian versions omit meat, and instead mashed potatoes can be added to the dish.

Fried Chicken in Dried Molokhia and Roselle Leaves

A simple dish but with an odd combination - bitter and sour. It consists of chicken, dried molokhia and dried roselle leaves.

The preparation of the dish starts by sautéing chopped onion and green chilli in vegetable oil, then adding chicken pieces, turmeric powder, ginger garlic paste, salt and lime juice. All are mixed

fried chicken in dried molokhia and roselle leaves

then cooked, stirring occasionally, until the water from the meat is reduced and the oil starts separating. The dried roselle and dried molokhia leaves are added, mixed in and stir-fried before adding more lime juice.

This dish is served with plain rice.

Variations include using different types of vegetable oil.

Rolled Molokhia

This is a Manipuri delicacy, and it looks similar to Middle Eastern, Greek or Turkish stuffed vine leaves – but it absolutely does not taste the same.

preparation of rolled molokhia

The preparation is labour-intensive. Chopped shrimp, chives, green chili, fresh coriander leaves, ginger, cumin powder, asafoetida, besan (chickpea flour) and salt to taste are mixed. The molokhia leaves are laid out, the mix is put in small amounts over them, they are rolled and fried.

rolled molokhia

It is often served as a starter with green salad and tomato sauce.

Southeast Asian Cuisines

Once again, the molokhia plant is commonly found in several countries in Southeast Asia region. It is cultivated both commercially and in the wild, but the majority of its usage is mostly for industrial rather than culinary purposes.

The country where molokhia is considered a major culinary ingredient is the Philippines, particularly in the Ilocos Region in northwestern Luzon, and Western Visayas. The vegetable is used extensively and has a huge variety of dishes, where the vegetable is used either as a main or complimentary ingredient. The plant grows wild and is used in several stews as either a main ingredient or one of many ingredients. It is often cooked fresh. In Vietnam and Thailand, it is used less often, traditionally in only few recipes. It is used to a lesser extent in the rest of Southeastern Asia.

Below I describe some of the more popular dishes where molokhia is utilised as a major ingredient. These dishes come from several locations in the region, but many of them come from the Philippines. As with other regions, many dishes have evolved over time and new ones are emerging with advancement of cooking methods.

Thus, we also present some newly created dishes. As with the practice adopted in the previous sections, the dishes are mentioned in descriptive names, rather than local names, since the names are often referred to in the local languages. In certain instances, a local name is used if it is widely known.

Molokhia Vegetable and Fish Soup (Dinengdeng)

Dinengdeng (also called inabraw) is a famous regional Filipino dish in the Ilocos region in the Philippines. The name is incorrectly used, sometimes interchangeably, with another equally famous dish called pinakbet. Both are fermented fish (salted anchovies), soup-based dishes. The former contains fewer vegetables and more fermented fish than the latter. The dish often includes smoked fish and vegetables. Several of its recipes include molokhia leaves as a major ingredient. The bulanglang recipe in the Southern Tagalog region is very similar.

molokhia vegetable and fish soup (dinengdeng)

The preparation of the dish is simple, despite it containing many ingredients. The easiest way to cook dinengdeng is to put all the ingredients together in one pot and cook everything at the same time. But for better texture, it is preferable to add the vegetables that take longer to cook first, and then place the green leafy ones into the pot shortly after. It starts with boiling water, then adding the chopped onions, ginger, and tomatoes, then the harder vegetables- such as chopped and sliced bitter melon, green beans, squash, okra and bagoong.[36] Smoked or grilled fish comes next, followed by softer

---

[36] Bagoong is a Filipino condiment made of either fermented fish or krill or shrimp paste with salt.

vegetables, which include molokhia and red spinach, later, all is simmered till tender.

It is served with plain rice.

Variations include adding additional sauces, spices - such as taps (fish sauce) and black pepper; not adding fish; using pork instead of fish; using any available vegetables and leaves, such as bok choy, mushrooms, green papaya, bamboo shoots or even lubeg (a type of Filipino cherry).

A related dish is called laswa, which is an Ilonggo boiled vegetable soup, similar to the dinengdeng of Ilocos. However, laswa is mostly seasoned with salt, while dinengdeng is flavoured with bagoong. Apart from this, the preparation process is very similar and so is the serving.

Molokhia Stew (Saluyot Adobong)

Adobo is considered the unofficial national dish of the Philippines, which is a stew often contains meat, seafood, or vegetables marinated with vinegar, soy sauce or patis (fish sauce), garlic, black peppercorns and bay leaves. This version includes molokhia leaves as a major ingredient. Similar recipes are called paksiw, where only vinegar is used.

molokhia stew (saluyot adobong)

In its simplest version, the dish uses molokhia as the main ingredient, but other common recipes include using additional vegetables such as green beans, water spinach and also adding fish or shrimps. The preparation starts by having chopped onion, garlic and tomatoes sautéed in vegetable oil then adding soy sauce, vinegar, fish sauce and salt and black pepper to taste, then adding the molokhia leaves and cooking till tender.

It is served with plain rice.

Variations include adding pork or chicken, shrimps or sardines, or adding additional or alternative vegetables.

Molokhia and Bamboo Shoots and Coconut Milk Stew (Ginataang Labong at Saluyot)

The term ginataang refers to dishes in the Filipino cuisine which are cooked with coconut milk. Numerous vegetables are cooked this way. This version includes whole molokhia leaves and bamboo shoots, which is very common in Eastern and Southeastern Asian cuisines.

molokhia and bamboo shoots and coconut milk stew (ginataang labong at saluyot)

The preparation is simple if using tinned bamboo shoots, otherwise the shoots need to be pre-boiled to remove the toxins present in it. The bamboo shoots are sautéed in boiling water with chopped onion, garlic, ginger, patis, salt and pepper to taste. The molokhia leaves and other ingredients are cooked till tender and then the coconut milk is added.

The dish is served with plain rice.

Variations include adding dried anchovies, crab or shrimps; adding red or green chilli for spicier version; adding other vegetables, instead of the bamboo shoots, such as bilimbi.[37]

Molokhia and Coconut Milk Stew (Saluyot Laing)

Laing, is a Filipino dish of shredded leafy vegetables with meat or seafood, cooked in thick coconut milk and spices. It originates from the Bicol Region in the Philippines. It is sometimes called pinangat. Technically, laing is also a type of ginataang and thus may also be referred to as ginataang laing. In this version, molokhia leaves are the main vegetable.

molokhia and coconut milk stew (saluyot laing)

Sauté chopped onion, garlic, ginger, green chilli, dried red chilli or chilli powder and shredded dried fish in vegetable oil. Add coconut milk and

---

[37] An extremely sour fruit native to Southeast Asia.

bring the mix to a boil, then dried molokhia leaves are added, with salt and black pepper to taste and the mix continues to cook, with an added bouillon cube or shrimp paste on low heat towards the end of the cooking process.

The dish is served with boiled white rice as a vegetable side to complement meat or fish side dishes.

Variations include using other vegetables such as taro leaves, or omitting the fish for a vegetarian version. Also, fish can be substituted with shrimps, crabs, pork or chicken as preferred.

Stir-Fry Molokhia (Ginisang Saluyot)

The term ginisang refers to stir-fry in Tagalog, not to be confused with ginisang munggo, which refers to a savory mung bean soup. This is a simple dish that contains whole molokhia leaves.

stir-fry molokhia (ginisang saluyot)

The preparation is quick. Here, chopped onion, garlic, tomatoes are stir-fried in vegetable oil, salt to taste and soy sauce are added, then the molokhia leaves and fried till tender.

The dish is served with plain rice.

Variations include adding fried fish or other vegetables, such as mung beans, okra and peppers, or adding red or green chilli for a spicier version.

Fried Molokhia Leaves (Tortang Saluyot)

A simple snack, where whole molokhia leaves are dipped in batter, battered and then fried. This is similar to the way it is done in Bengal and Assam, but with added eggs and different spices. Here the eggs are mixed with minced garlic, ground pepper, and oregano, then each molokhia leaf is dipped in the mix, then in whole flour, which is optionally mixed with bouillon cube and salt to taste before being deep fried.

fried molokhia leaves (tortang saluyot)

Variations include adding tuna into the mix.

Molokhia Burger

A modern Filipino recipe that creates vegetarian molokhia patties.

molokhia burger

The preparation is simple, here the molokhia leaves are mixed with minced garlic, minced onion, sugar, salt and ground pepper. They are combined with egg and flour until the mixture achieves a dough-like consistency, then it is shaped into burger patties and fried until golden brown.

It is served as a burger substitute in sandwiches or as main dish.

Molokhia Salad

A simple modern Filipino dish using whole molokhia leaves.

molokhia salad

The preparation is simple, where ginger, onions and tomatoes are chopped, then mixed with vinegar, sugar, lemon juice and salt to taste. Blanched molokhia leaves are added and all are combined.

The dish is served as an appetizer or a side dish.

Variations to the dish include making it spicier by adding chilli or chilli powder.

Filipino Creative Experimentation

Lately food enthusiasts are experimenting with new ways to use molokhia leaves where it is being incorporated into food products and into the healthy life-style trend.

Most of the following products use dried powdered molokhia leaves as an ingredient in well-known food products. Examples include:

1. Saluyot cookies.

saluyot cookies

2. Saluyot instant noodles

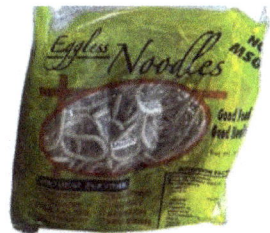

saluyot instant noodles

3. Saluyot pasta.

saluyot pasta

4. Saluyot cheese spread.

saluyot cheese spread

5. Saluyot chips.

saluyot chips

6. Saluyot juice, which juices fresh leaves and often uses it as part of a mix vegetable and fruit juice.

saluyot juice

Molokhia Crab Soup (Canh cua rau đay)

A refreshing Vietnamese soup made of crab meat, chopped molokhia leaves and other vegetables.

molokhia crab soup (canh cua rau đay)

The soup preparation involves two steps. First, if using fresh crabs, the crab meat needs to be extracted from the shell and claws, this process can be simplified by using pre-prepared meat. Second, a simple cooking process is done, where the minced crab meat is boiled, this is followed by peeled, chopped luffah gourd and then the chopped molokhia leaves. The mixture is stirred until cooked, with salt and soup powder added to taste.[38]

It is often served alongside other vegetable dishes such as salted aubergine (eggplant), salted tomatoes or braised meat.

Variations can often include substituting crab with shrimp (fresh or dried), omitting the gourd, adding chopped spinach, sautéed chopped onions or adding extra flavouring, including fish sauce and vinegar or MSG[39].

Thai Stir-Fry Molokhia

A simple dish, less sophisticated compared to its Chinese counterpart, comprised of molokhia and garlic.

Preparing the dish is very simple, minced garlic is fried and set aside, the

---

[38] Soup powder is a combination of spices. Mainly: salt, sugar, pepper powder, chilli powder, dried scallions, garlic powder and flavour enhancers.

[39] Monosodium glutamate (MSG), also known as sodium glutamate, is the sodium salt of glutamic acid. MSG is found naturally in some foods including tomatoes and cheese] MSG is used in cooking as a flavor enhancer with a savory taste that intensifies the meaty, savory flavor of food.

whole molokhia leaves are stir-fried in the same oil, salted to taste, until dry. Then the fried garlic is sprinkled on top.

The dish is served with plain white rice congee (i.e. type of porridge).

Thai stir-fry molokhia

Variations might be substituting garlic with soy paste, textured vegetable protein or minced pork.[40]

---

[40] Textured or texturized vegetable protein (TVP), also known as textured soy protein (TSP), soy meat, or soya chunks is a defatted soy flour product, a by-product of extracting soybean oil. It is often used as a meat analogue or meat extender. It is quick to cook, with a protein content comparable to certain meats.

East Asian Cuisines

Although the plant is widely available in several countries in the region where it is cultivated commercially, actually the majority of its usage is for industrial purposes.

In East Asia, following the decline in its industrial use, the molokhia plant is increasingly utilised for culinary purposes. Currently it is a major ingredient only in a few parts of China, namely in the region of Chaoshan, in Guangdong, South China, also in one region in Taiwan, namely Taichung. Its use in cooking in the rest of China and Taiwan is not common but it is increasing.

In Japan, the use of molokhia was rare, but it appears that the country has discovered and found a revelation in molokhia in the last two decades and its use in culinary circuits is gaining considerable momentum.

The situation in Korea mirrors the early stages of Japan's usage i.e. used as a herb or a nutritional supplement where it is often sold in dried powder packs or jars or supplement tablets. They are also sold as tea bags.

Below I describe some of the more popular dishes where molokhia is utilised as a key ingredient. These dishes come from several locations in the region, but many of them come from China and Taiwan. As with other regions, many dishes evolved over time and new ones emerged with advancement of cooking methods. Thus, I present some new creative dishes, most of which originate in Japan. Some of which has been repeated several times on the internet – a testament that they are being slowly adopted as new ways of cooking.

As before, in the previous sections, the following dishes are given descriptive names rather than colloquial names, since the names are often referred to in local dialects. In certain instances, a local name is used if it is widely known.

Chinese Stir-Fry Molokhia

This popular simple dish from Chaoshan, Guangdong, in Southern China, is made with molokhia leaves and garlic.

Chinese stir-fry molokhia

The preparation of this dish is simple. It starts with sautéing minced garlic in oil, then adding washed and drained whole molokhia leaves, soy (or fermented) sauce, bean paste, salt and pepper to taste, then the leaves are stir-fried until dry.

The dish is served with porridge, pickles, or sometimes boiled white rice and dried radish

Variations of the dish include boiling or blanching the molokhia leaves before stir-frying them and adding chicken essence[41].

A simpler variation is to eat stir-fry molokhia as a snack, where the washed and drained whole molokhia leaves are stir-fried with added salt till dry and then eaten.

---

[41] Essence of chicken is a liquid derived from cooking whole chickens down into a liquid. Any animal fats are generally removed to produce a liquid that contains little or no cholesterol.

Stir-Fry Pork with Molokhia

A simple Chinese dish made of diced or pork with molokhia leaves.

stir-fry pork with molokhia

The dish preparation starts by cooking the pork in a pressure cooker; stir-fry chopped onion, chopped red chillies, minced garlic and then the pork, adding salt to taste. Mix with Chinese rice wine vinegar, soya sauce, and oyster sauce Then the whole molokhia leaves are added and stir-fried to the mix.

It is served with boiled white rice.

Variations to the dish include using minced pork, or more recently using chicken instead of pork.

Molokhia with Pork and Century Egg Soup

Based on a traditional Chinese recipe, this dish is a soup that combines pork, century old egg or preserved egg[42] and molokhia leaf.

molokhia with pork and century egg soup

The preparation process is simple. Start by marinating minced pork in soy

---

[42] Century eggs, also known as preserved eggs, are a Chinese egg-based culinary dish made by preserving duck, chicken or quail eggs in a mixture of clay, ash, salt, quicklime, and rice hulls for several weeks to several months, depending on the method of processing, where the yolk becomes a dark green to grey color, with a creamy

sauce, sesame oil, Chinese wine and corn flour. Water is brought to boil, the minced pork is added first, followed by the whole molokhia leaves. The preserved eggs are added just before the end and salt is added to taste.

Variations to the dish include substituting the pork with chicken, or even using spinach instead of molokhia. Also, for vegetarians, wolfberry[43] can be added to the recipe instead of pork and eggs.

The soup is often served with boiled rice, or by adding noodles to it.

Rolled Egg and Molokhia

A side dish made of eggs, molokhia and carrots, that resembles the traditional omelettes.

rolled egg and molokhia

The preparation is simple. Eggs are cracked, mixed with pepper and salt, add the chopped molokhia leaves and a small amount of chopped carrots. Mix all the ingredients thoroughly. Preheat a pan, add cooking oil, and add the mixture. Once the omelette is cooked then roll up the egg crust. Garnish as desired.

consistency and strong flavor, while the white becomes a dark brown, translucent jelly with a salty flavour.

43 Wolfberry, also known as goji berry, is a sweet, nutritious fruit that comes from the Lycium barbarum or Lycium chinense shrubs.

Molokhia Cake

A traditional sweet dish from Ninghua in Fujian, China, made from rice and molokhia leaves.

molokhia cake

The dish is made by beating soaked rice, washed molokhia leaves and water with a wooden shovel, and then adding an appropriate amount of sugar to fully mix and bond them to form green bun balls, which are then kneaded into small pieces and steamed.

The green buns are served as a sweet snack or dessert.

Main variation to this dish is to use ramie[44] leaves instead of molokhia, which is the actual traditional recipe. Another variation is to fry the balls in camellia oil instead of steaming.

Molokhia Soup (Ma Yi Soup)

A traditional soup in Taichung, Taiwan, made from young molokhia leaves, dried fish and sweet potatoes. It is

considered the regional signature dish,

---

[44] Ramie is a flowering plant in the nettle family Urticaceae, native to Eastern Asia.

and is gaining popularity on the island.

The preparation of the soup is not easy. The young molokhia leaves of jute are used for the soup, and they will go through four steps: picking to remove all the stems and veins, then placing them in a laundry bag and rubbing for 10-20 minutes, then kneading to squeeze the liquid, and then washing to remove the bitter taste. Add cubed sweet potatoes to boiling water and baking soda, followed by the molokhia leaves and then the dried fish (whitebait) and a little bit of Taibai powder[45] to thicken them; cook for few minutes, with salt and bonito powder[46] added to taste.

molokhia soup (ma yi soup)

It can be served cold or hot as a soup or over plain white rice.

Variations include skipping the sweet potatoes or the dried fish, but not both, or substituting whitebait with anchovies.

Fried Battered Molokhia

A simple snack eaten in Taichung, Taiwan, where whole molokhia leaves are dipped in batter and then fried. This is similar to the way done in Bengal and Assam, or in the Philippines mentioned

---

[45] Taibi powder is a thickening starch.
[46] Bonito powder is a seasoning made of finely ground dried fish, popular in Japanese cuisine.

earlier.

Taiwanese Creative Experimentation

The district of Nantun in Taichung, Taiwan hosts the 'Nantun Jute Art Culture Museum – Litoudian', which is dedicated to the history of the jute (i.e. molokhia) cultivation in the region, and its industrial and culinary uses. As part of its activities, the local cultural teams are actively working with bakeries in the area of the development of new molokhia products.

Most of these products use dried powdered molokhia leaves as an ingredient into well-known food products. Examples include:

1. Molokhia cakes, which include versions of traditional steamed rice cake with fillings, suncakes,[47] mooncakes[48] and steamed buns.

molokhia cakes varieties

---

[47] Suncake is a popular Taiwanese dessert originally from the city of Taichung. The typical fillings consist of maltose (condensed malt sugar), and they are usually sold in special gift boxes as souvenirs for visitors.
[48] Mooncake is a Chinese dessert traditionally eaten during the Mid-Autumn Festival. A typical mooncake is a round pastry, that has a rich thick filling usually made from red bean paste or lotus seed paste.

2. Molokhia bread loafs.

molokhia bread loaf

3. Molokhia sweet biscuits.

molokhia biscuit

4. Molokhia nougat candies.

molokhia nougat candies

5. Molokhia ice cream in scoops or in bao.[49]

molokhia ice cream

---

[49] A bao is a plain steamed dumpling which is often compared to bread.

6. Molokhia popsicles.

molokhia popsicles

7. Molokhia milk tea.

molokhia milk tea

The traditional methods of preparing the above edible products are used with molokhia dried powder added to the flour or milk.

Molokhia in Traditional Japanese Recipes

Molokhia is not native to Japan and was introduced to the country in the 1980s, where it is called in the Japanese cuisine either moroheiya (モロヘイヤ) or shimatsunaso (シマツナソ). Since then, the leafy vegetable has found numerous uses as a substitute to other leafy vegetables in many traditional Japanese recipes. It gained popularity due to its character as a thickening agent. It is also used as a herb.

Currently it is used as a main or complementary ingredient in soups, tempura, and salads. A simple search on Cookpad listed hundreds of recipes covering all types of Japanese dishes. Examples are shown below.

1. Molokhia Soup, in many varieties, such as miso soup or the soup is poured over boiled gyoza.

molokhia soup

2. Molokhia Salad, in several varieties, used raw with other vegetables such as tomatoes or served as ohitashi, where the leaves are blanched.

molokhia salad

3. Molokhia Tempura, eaten often as a side dish.

Molokhia Tempura

4. Molokhia Bonito, which is a side dish made of molokhia and tuna flakes.

molokhia bonito

5. Molokhia with natto.[50], which is a side dish often eaten with noodles.

molokhia with natto

6. Chicken Teriyaki with Molokhia Sauce, as a main dish.

chicken teriyaki with molokhia sauce

7. Stir-Fried Molokhia, with other vegetables, chicken or eggs, etc.

stir-fried molokhia

8. Green curry with molokhia.

green curry with molokhia

I am not expanding into describing the preparation of these dishes as this will

---

[50] Natto is a traditional Japanese food made from fermented whole soybeans.

lead to writing-up a Japanese cookbook since the vegetable found its way to numerous dishes. Interested readers can find these recipes in many books or online.

Japanese Creative Experimentation

Besides usage in traditional recipes, Japanese chefs and incorporated food industry experts molokhia into numerous products, utilising the powdered form as their main raw material. Many of these ideas have already been described when discussing Filipino creative experimentation earlier. These include.

1. Molokhia noodles.

molokhia noodles

2. Pickled molokhia in soy sauce.

pickled molokhia

3. Molokhia cookies or sweet

biscuits.

4. Molokhia juice, fresh or made from powder with other juices.

molokhia juice

5. Flavoured tea, that contains molokhia.

6. Extraction as a sushi wrap.

Molokhia Entry to Korean Food

Similar to Japan, molokhia is not native to Korea and was introduced only recently following the same path in Japan but at earlier stages. Since then, the leafy vegetable found few uses as a substitute or in addition to other leafy vegetables in some traditional recipes. It is also slowly gaining popularity due to its characters as a thickening agent. Also, it may be used as a herb.

molokhia and kimchi in hot pot

Here again, I am not going to describe traditional Korean cooking. One example I show is where it has been used in a pairing with kimchi in a hot pot.

Caribbean Cuisine

The Caribbean cuisine is famous for being influenced by many international cuisines and for including many fresh and seafood ingredients. While exploring the cuisine I note that molokhia is a main ingredient in one country, namely Haiti, where it is known as lalo, and is used in one famous recipe with numerous variations.

Surprisingly the leafy vegetable is not common in the Dominican Republic, which shares the island of Hispaniola with Haiti.

Other leafy greens are widespread in the rest of the Caribbean, and some are sometimes mistakenly confused with molokhia. The most famous is the dish callaloo (many spelling variations exist), which uses different leafy vegetables, such as amaranth in Jamaica, taro leaves in Trinidad, or Xanthosoma in Puerto Rico.

The traditional Haitian dish is described below. As with other regions, it evolved over time and with advancement of cooking methods. We note some new creative variations, most of which created by the Haitian diaspora in the United States. Some of which has been repeated several times on the internet – a testament that they are being slowly adopted as new ways of cooking.

Molokhia Stew (Lalo Legim)

A traditional Haitian stew originates in the region of L'Artibonite, located in the centre of Haiti, but spread to the whole country and is also popular by Haitian diaspora in the USA and France.

molokhia stew (lalo legim)

Traditionally, the dish is a stew made of molokhia leaves, spinach, with beef, and blue crab.

The preparation process is a multi-step, starting with the cleaning of blue crabs with lemon juice or lime, seasoning them with salt, pepper and lemon juice and refrigerate till used later, or boil and set aside to use later. The diced beef is marinated with lime or lemon juice and is flavoured with herbs and spices including garlic, onion, thyme, rosemary, scallions, parsley, salt, black pepper, ground cloves, chicken bouillon or beef bouillon, and Epis.[51] It can also be cooked till tender beforehand and set aside. The coarsely chopped dried molokhia leaves are soaked in water and baking soda to reduce the sliminess or gooiness, but frozen or fresh leaves can also be used.

Numerous recipes are found online that differ when the meat, seafood and green

---

[51] Epis is Epis is a blend of peppers, garlic, Bell peppers, garlic, citrus juice, vinegar, parsley, and other herbs and spices that is used in Haitian cuisine.

leaves are added together. In essence, tomato paste, and diced bell pepper are sautéed in a pot with olive oil (or other vegetable oil). The marinated beef (or cooked beef) is then added to the pot with hot pepper or hot paste, then the strained molokhia leaves (or frozen leaves) and the chopped spinach leaves are added. Optionally watercress and chopped tomatoes can be added also. All is slow cooked together covered in aluminium foil in a covered pot till beef is thoroughly cooked.[52] The crab is then added, and the mixture is cooked further till ready. Note that in some variations crab is added at the same time as the beef. Finally, some habanero or cayenne pepper can be added to taste.

The stew is often served with white rice and pigeon bean sauce (known as sos pwa), or recently with boiled root vegetables or other grain dishes.

Variations to the traditional recipe can use only seafood without any meat, and use conch or shrimps besides or instead of crabs. Also, other types of meat can be used added to beef such as cow foot, beef intestines, diced pork, pig foot or pig tail. New variations also use turkey meat instead of beef. Surprisingly, I could not find recipes with chicken. Cooking times differ depending on the type of meat or if seafood is being used.

---

[52] May need to add some water, but minimal.

Furthermore, vegetarian versions of the dish are now being cooked where vegetable bouillon is used, also diced carrots can be added.

While going through numerous recipes published online, one interesting recommendation is to use a wooden spoon rather than metal, apparently this affects the texture of the dish.

Rest of the World Cuisines

Molokhia is cultivated widely in Brazil, but it is overwhelmingly used for industrial uses as a source of fibre. I could not identify traditional use for culinary purposes there, or in the rest of South and Central America.

Likewise, I did not find culinary uses in Mexico.

Despite the plant being known as a source of fibre for industrial uses throughout Europe, it never made the leap into use as an edible ingredient into traditional recipes. Obviously, with the world's populations mass movement since the 1950s, and the recent trends in the homogenisation of cuisines, and with so many recipes crossing borders, the use of molokhia as an ingredient is increasing, due to the presence of significant Middle Eastern and African minorities across the continent.

Similarly, the trends are repeating in the United States and Canada with the ingredient being spread by Middle Eastern, Haitian, Filipino and African immigrants.

Also, Middle Eastern and Filipino

immigrants spread the same trend to Australia and New Zealand.

Recently, we have seen some modern uses of the ingredient by Western chefs. In the next section I mention few examples that fall under modern global cuisine heading.

Creative Fusion Dishes

There is a huge trend on the internet showcasing many new recipes and fusion cooking. For molokhia, this seems a bit less that others – maybe due to its nature or sliminess.

Some are universal modern recipes that cannot be characterised under traditional geographic cuisines. And some are just restaurant posh recipes.[53,54]

Examples of fusion recipes include:

1. Egg roll with molokhia.

egg roll with molokhia

2. Omelette

omelette

---

[53] https://www.instagram.com/p/CG3vCUOH-7r/ from Toyo Eatery
[54] https://www.facebook.com/OfficialSabrinas Kitchen/photos/turmeric-cumin-chori-rice-in-saluyot-wrapsrecipeingredients1-bunch-saluyot-leave/2063300273712039/?_rdr from Sabrinas

3. Pasta with molokhia and smoked salmon.

Pasta with molokhia and smoked salmon

4. Cold potage of molokhia and couscous.

cold potage of molokhia and couscous

5. Molokhia harissa, a Saudi dip.

molokhia harissa

6. Middle Eastern chicken breasts stuffed with molokhia.

Middle Eastern chicken breasts stuffed with molokhia

7. Japanese bagged grilled tuna and molokhia.

bagged grilled tuna and molokhia

8. Japanese oyster chowder with molokhia.

oyster chowder with molokhia

9. Quiche with molokhia.

quiche with molokhia

10. Molokhia cake.

Molokhia cake

www.ingramcontent.com/pod-product-compliance
Lightning Source LLC
Chambersburg PA
CBHW060411090426
42734CB00011B/2282